D0984254

Little Deeds of Kindness

of

Kindness

Edited by Jill Wolf
ISBN 0-7824-8050-0
Copyright © 1996 Antioch Publishing

Antioch Publishing
Yellow Springs, Ohio 45387
Printed in the U.S.A.

Do a deed of simple kindness;
Though its end you may not see,
It may reach, like widening ripples,
Down a long eternity.

—Joseph Norris

CONTENTS

Shall we make a new rule of life from tonight:
always to try to be a little kinder than is necessary?
—J. M. Barrie

A kind heart is a fountain of gladness, making
everything in its vicinity freshen into smiles.
—Washington Irving

In this world, you must be a bit too kind in order
to be kind enough.

—Author Unknown

 A New Rule of Life

Little deeds of kindness,
   little words of love,
Help to make earth happy
   like the heaven above.
        —Julia Fletcher Carney

In some loving acts of kindness
As they show how much they care—
In the lives of folk around me
I find God reflected there.

        —Cyrus E. Albertson

How beautiful a day can be when kindness touches it.

—George Elliston

All the beautiful sentiments in the world weigh less than a single lovely action.

—James Russell Lowell

Kind hearts are more than coronets. . . .

—Alfred, Lord Tennyson

Always, Sir, set a high value on spontaneous kindness.

—Samuel Johnson

What wisdom can you find that is greater than kindness?

—Jean Jacques Rousseau

That best portion of
a good man's life,—
His little, nameless,
unremembered acts
Of kindness and love.
—William Wordsworth

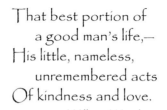

True worth is in being, not seeming;
In doing each day that goes by
Some little good—not in the dreaming
Of great things to do by-and-by.
For whatever men say in blindness,
And spite of the fancies of youth,
There's nothing so kingly as kindness,
And nothing so royal as truth.
—Alice Cary

If you sit down at set of sun
And count the acts that you have done,
And, counting find
One self-denying deed, one word
That eased the heart of him who heard;
One glance most kind,
That fell like sunshine where it went—
Then you may count that day well spent.

—George Eliot

Kindness: what a strange word to find on anybody's lips these days. It is like a style in clothes which is no longer worn, or like a musty language no longer spoken . . . . Nevertheless, it has a way of returning every now and then to earth . . . . and there is kindness again, nestling stubbornly in people's hearts, lifting a small peaceful voice, ready for the millennium.

—Robert Nathan

What do we live for, if it is not to make life less difficult to each other?

—George Eliot

. . . always try to be kind to each other and everyone else.

1 Thessalonians 5:15 (NIV)

Let me be a little kinder,
Let me be a little blinder
To the faults of those about me;
Let me praise a little more;
Let me be, when I am weary,
Just a little bit more cheery;
Let me serve a little better
Those that I am striving for.
                          —Author Unknown

If the world seems cold to you,
Kindle fires to warm it!
                          —Lucy Larcom

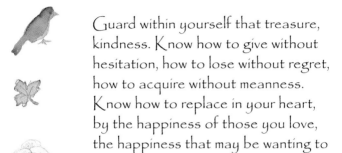

Guard within yourself that treasure,
kindness. Know how to give without
hesitation, how to lose without regret,
how to acquire without meanness.
Know how to replace in your heart,
by the happiness of those you love,
the happiness that may be wanting to
yourself.

—George Sand

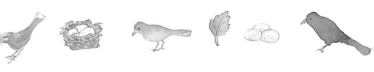

Shall we make a new rule of life from tonight: always to try to be a little kinder than is necessary?
—J. M. Barrie

. . . just the art of being kind
Is all this sad world needs.
—Ella Wheeler Wilcox

Life is short. Let us make haste to be kind.

—Henri Amiel

You cannot do a kindness too soon, because you never know how soon it will be too late.

—Proverb

Strew gladness on the paths of men—
You will not pass this way again.

—Sam Walter Foss

I shall pass through this world but once. If, therefore, there be any kindness I can show, or any good thing I can do, let me do it now; let me not defer it or neglect it, for I shall not pass this way again.

—Étienne de Grellet

Take time to do the little things
Which leave the satisfactory thought,
When other joys have taken wings,
That we have labored as we ought;
That in a world where all contend,
We often stopped to be a friend.

—Edgar A. Guest

Life is too brief
Between the budding and the falling leaf,
Between the seed time and the golden sheaf,
For hate and spite.
We have no time for malice and for greed;
Therefore, with love make beautiful the deed;
Fast speeds the night.

—W. M. Vories

PASS IT ON

If we were to make the conscious and frequent effort of treating others with consideration, the effects on us and on society as a whole would be amazing.
—Henry Charles Link

Perfect obedience to the law of kindness would abolish government and the State.
—Octavius Frothingham

Nobody is kind only to one person at once, but to many persons in one.
—Frederick W. Faber

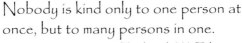

How far that little candle throws
    his beams!
So shines a good deed in a
    naughty world.
                —William Shakespeare

Kindness gives birth to kindness.
                —Sophocles

When I see a deed of kindness,
I am eager to be kind.
                —Edgar A. Guest

17

A good deed is never lost; he who sows courtesy reaps friendship, and he who plants kindness gathers love.

—St. Basil

Sow good services; sweet remembrances will grow from them.

—Madame de Stael

In scattering the seed . . . your kind deeds, you are giving away in one form or another, part of your personality, and taking into yourself part of another. He who has received them from you will hand them on to another. And how can you tell what part you may have in the future determination of the destinies of humanity?

—Fyodor Dostoevsky

Influence

Drop a pebble in the water,
And its ripples reach out far;
And the sunbeams dancing on them
May reflect them to a star.

Give a smile to someone passing,
Thereby make his morning glad;
It may greet you in the evening
When your own heart may be sad.

Do a deed of simple kindness;
Though its end you may not see,
It may reach, like widening ripples,
Down a long eternity.

                              —Joseph Norris

Pass It On

Have you had a kindness shown?
Pass it on.
'Twas not given for thee alone,
Pass it on.
Let it travel down the years,
Let it wipe another's tears,
Till in heav'n the deed appears—
Pass it on.

Did you hear the loving word?
Pass it on.
Like the singing of a bird?
Pass it on.
Let its music live and grow,
Let it cheer another's woe;
You have reaped what others sow—
Pass it on.

'Twas the sunshine of a smile—
Pass it on.
Staying but a little while!
Pass it on.
April beam a little thing,
Still it wakes the flowers of spring,
Makes the silent birds to sing—
Pass it on.

—Henry Burton

One can never pay in gratitude; one
can only pay "in kind" somewhere else
in life.

—Anne Morrow Lindbergh

 For whoever knows how to return a
kindness he has received must be a
friend above all price.

—Sophocles

 One of the most difficult things to
give away is kindness, for it is usually
returned.

—Author Unknown

 There is as much greatness of mind
in acknowledging a good turn as in
doing it.

—Seneca

The Kindly Neighbor

I have a kindly neighbor, one who stands
Beside my gate and chats with me awhile,
Gives me the glory of his radiant smile
And comes at times to help with willing hands.
No station high or rank this man commands;
He, too, must trudge, as I, the long day's mile;
And yet, devoid of pomp or gaudy style,
He has a worth exceeding stocks or lands.

To him I go when sorrow's at my door;
On him I lean when burdens come my way;
Together oft we talk our trials o'er,
And there is warmth in each good-night we say.
A kindly neighbor! Wars and strife shall end
When man has made the man next door his friend.

—Edgar A. Guest

Let me live in my house by the side of the road
And be a friend of man.

—Sam Walter Foss

Human kindness has never weakened the stamina or softened the fiber of a free people. A nation does not have to be cruel in order to be tough.

—Franklin Delano Roosevelt

If a man be gracious to strangers, it shows that he is a citizen of the world, and his heart is no island, cut off from other islands, but a continent that joins them.

—Francis Bacon

It is good to give a stranger a meal, or a night's lodging. It is better to be hospitable to his good meaning and thought, and give courage to a companion. We must be as courteous to a man as we are to a picture, which we are willing to give the advantage of a good light.

—Ralph Waldo Emerson

Do not forget to entertain strangers, for by so doing some people have entertained angels without knowing it.

Hebrews 13:2 (NIV)

I have had that curiously *symbolical* and reassuring pleasure, of being entertained with overflowing and simple kindness by a family of totally unknown people—an adventure which will always bring home to me the goodwill of the world.

—Arthur C. Benson

It is a good and safe rule to sojourn in every place, as if you meant to spend your life there, never omitting an opportunity of doing a kindness, or speaking a true word, or making a friend.

—John Ruskin

We are all travellers in the wilderness of this world, and the best that we find in our travels is an honest friend.

—Robert Louis Stevenson

Many a friendship, long, loyal, and self-sacrificing, rested at first on no thicker a foundation than a kind word.

—Frederick W. Faber

We cannot tell the precise moment when friendship is formed. As in filling a vessel drop by drop, there is at last a drop which makes it run over; so in a series of kindnesses there is at last one which makes the heart run over.

—Samuel Johnson

The Good Samaritan

A certain man went down from Jerusalem to Jericho, and fell among thieves, who stripped him of his clothing, wounded him, and departed, leaving him half dead.

Now by chance a certain priest came down that road. And when he saw him, he passed by on the other side.

Likewise a Levite, when he arrived at the place, came and looked, and passed by on the other side.

But a certain Samaritan, as he journeyed, came where he was. And when he saw him, had compassion on him, and went to him and bandaged his wounds, pouring on oil and wine; and he set him on his own animal, brought him to an inn, and took care of him.

On the next day, when he departed, he took out two denarii, gave them to the innkeeper, and said to him, "Take care of him; and whatever more you spend, when I come again, I will repay you."

Luke 10:30-35 (NKJV)

Love all God's creation, both the whole and
every grain of sand. Love every leaf, every ray
of light. Love the animals, love the plants, love
each separate thing.

—Fyodor Dostoevsky

Hurt no living thing:
Ladybird, no butterfly,
Nor moth with dusty wing,
No cricket chirping cheerily,
Nor grasshopper so light of leap,
Nor dancing gnat, no beetle fat,
Nor harmless worms that creep.

—Christina Rossetti

He that planteth a tree is a servant of God,
He provideth a kindness for many generations,
And faces that he hath not seen shall bless him.

—Henry van Dyke

What sunshine is to flowers, smiles are to humanity.

—Joseph Addison

A kind heart is a fountain of gladness, making everything in its vicinity freshen into smiles.

—Washington Irving

Wear a smile and have friends; wear a scowl and have wrinkles.

—George Eliot

The happiness of life is made of minute fractions . . . a kiss or smile, a kind look, a heartfelt compliment . . . .

—Samuel Taylor Coleridge

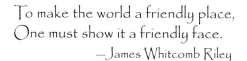

To make the world a friendly place,
One must show it a friendly face.
— James Whitcomb Riley

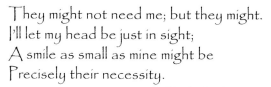

They might not need me; but they might.
I'll let my head be just in sight;
A smile as small as mine might be
Precisely their necessity.
— Emily Dickinson

A Smile

There's something you may give
A friend and stranger, too;
It seems that when you give it,
It's given back to you.

This gift is worth a million,
But doesn't cost a dime;
It's lasting in effect,
But doesn't take much time.

This simple little gesture
Can make the day worthwhile;
It's just as good as sunshine—
It's what we call a smile.

—Jill Wolf

A kind word is like a spring day.
—Russian Proverb

Wise sayings often fall on barren ground;
but a kind word is never thrown away.

—Sir Arthur Helps

Kind words prevent a good deal of that
perverseness which rough and imperious
usage often produces in generous minds.
—John Locke

She opens her mouth with wisdom, and on
her tongue is the law of kindness.
Proverbs 31:26 (NKJV)

In kindness and in gentleness our speech
Must carry messages of hope, and reach
The sweetest chords.
—W. M. Vories

Kind words produce their own image in men's souls; and a beautiful image it is. They soothe and quiet and comfort the hearer. They shame him out of his sour, morose, unkind feelings. We have not yet begun to use kind words in such abundance as they ought to be used.

—Blaise Pascal

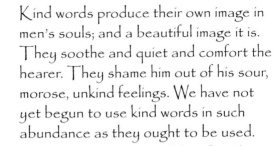

Do not keep the alabaster boxes of your love and tenderness sealed up until your friends are dead. Fill their lives with sweetness. Speak approving, cheering words while their ears can hear them, and while their hearts can be thrilled and made happier by them.

—George W. Childs

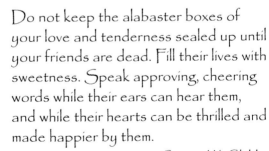

Whoever gives a small coin to a poor
man has six blessings bestowed upon
him, but he who speaks a kind word to
him obtains eleven blessings.

—from the Talmud

An anxious heart weighs a man down,
but a kind word cheers him up.

Proverbs 12:25 (NIV)

Kindness in words creates confi-
dence. Kindness in thinking creates
profoundness. Kindness in giving
creates love.

—Lao-tzu

Kind thoughts are rarer than either kind words or kind deeds. They imply a great deal of thinking about others. This in itself is rare. But they also imply a great deal of thinking about others without the thoughts being criticisms. This is rarer still.

—Frederick W. Faber

Of Courtesy, it is much less
Than Courage of Heart or Holiness,
Yet in my walks it seems to me
That the Grace of God is in Courtesy.

—Hilaire Belloc

A Breath of Kindness

Kindness consists in loving people more than they deserve.

—Joseph Joubert

Ask yourself daily, to how many ill-minded persons you have shown a kind disposition.

—Marcus Aurelius

The true and noble way to kill a foe, is not to kill him; you, with kindness, may so change him that he shall cease to be a foe, and then he's slain.

—Charles Aleyn

We cannot be just unless we are kindhearted.

—Luc de Clapiers

In this world, you must be a bit too kind in order to be kind enough.

—Author Unknown

Humane treatment may raise up one in whom the divine image has long been obscured. It is with the unfortunate, above all, that humane conduct is necessary.

—Fyodor Dostoevsky

True kindness presupposes the faculty of imagining as one's own the sufferings and joy of others. Without imagination, there can be weakness, theoretical or practical philanthropy, but not true kindness.

—André Gide

It is not written, blessed is he that *feedeth* the poor, but he that *considereth* the poor. A little thought and a little kindness are often worth more than a great deal of money.

—John Ruskin

My feeling is that there is nothing in life but refraining from hurting others, and comforting those that are sad.

—Olive Schreiner

. . . clothe yourselves with compassion, kindness, humility, gentleness and patience. Bear with each other and forgive whatever grievances you may have against one another. Forgive as the Lord forgave you. And over all these virtues put on love, which binds them together in perfect unity.

Colossians 3:12-14 (NIV)

Be kind and compassionate to one another, forgiving each other, just as in Christ God forgave you.

Ephesians 4:32 (NIV)

May I tell you why it seems to me a good thing for us to remember wrong that has been done us? That we may forgive it.

—Charles Dickens

If I can stop one heart from breaking,
I shall not live in vain;
If I can ease one life the aching,
Or cool one pain,
Or help one fainting robin
Unto his nest again,
I shall not live in vain.

     —Emily Dickinson

Every soul that touches yours—
Be it the slightest contact—
Gets therefrom some good;
Some little grace; one kindly thought;
One aspiration yet unfelt;
One bit of courage
For the darkening sky;
One gleam of faith
To brave the thickening ills of life;
One glimpse of brighter skies—
To make this life worthwhile
And heaven a surer heritage.

     —George Eliot

Oh, the comfort, the inexpressible comfort of feeling safe with a person, having neither to weigh thoughts nor measure words, but pouring them all right out, just as they are, chaff and grain together; certain that a faithful hand will take and sift them, keep what is worth keeping, and then with the breath of kindness blow the rest away.

—Dinah Maria Craik

I am thankful for your visit .... Like everyone else I feel the need of relations and friendship, of affection, of friendly intercourse, and I am not made of stone or iron, so I cannot miss these things without feeling ... a void and deep need. I tell you this to let you know how much good your visit has done me.

—Vincent van Gogh

Love has many ways of expressing itself, but in general the ways are two—the practical and the sentimental. Which is the higher and better way? It is merely a question of appropriateness under the circumstances. Love must express itself very often in coal, and cornmeal, and salt pork, and clothes. But let it not be concluded that love may not express itself in acts of pure sentiment. The soul has needs. Sympathy and tenderness and friendship are just as real and more enduring, than coal and wood. Sometimes a flower is more important than flour; sometimes a word of cheer is better than gold.

—Ferral

I would be kind, but kindness is not all:
In arid places may I find the wells,
The deeps within my neighbor's soul that call
To me, and lead me where his spirit dwells.
—Georgia Harkness

There are red-letter days in our lives when we
meet people who thrill us like a fine poem, people
whose handshake is brimful of unspoken sympathy and whose sweet, rich natures impart to our
eager, impatient spirits a wonderful restfulness
which is in its essence divine . . . . Perhaps we
never saw them before and they may never cross
our life's path again; but the influence of their
calm, mellow natures is a libation poured upon
our discontent, and we feel its healing touch as
the ocean feels the mountain stream freshening
its brine . . . .
—Helen Keller

Love is patient, love is kind.

1 Corinthians 13:4 (NIV)

It is not enough to love those who are near and dear to us. We must show them that we do so.

—Lord Avebury

The secret of happy marriage is simple: just keep on being as polite to each other as you are to your best friends.

—Robert Quillen

Don't flatter yourself that friendship authorizes you to say disagreeable things to your intimates. The nearer you come into relation with a person, the more necessary do tact and courtesy become.

—Oliver Wendell Holmes

 The balm of life, a kind and faithful friend.
—Mercy Otis Warren

 Like everything breathing of kindness—
Like these is the love of a friend.
—A. P. Stanley

 [Friends] cherish each other's hopes.
They are kind to each other's dreams.
—Henry David Thoreau

 With me her generosity and forbearance
were unfailing; patiently she consoled my
lunatic anxiety over adverse reviews, rejected
manuscripts, family ailments, and other minor
everyday annoyances which to her must have
seemed absurdly trivial.
—Vera Brittain, on a friend's kindness

Whenever I forget to notice any kindness of yours, do believe, my beloved friend, that I have, not withstanding, marked the date of it with a white stone, and also with a heart *not* of stone . . . .
    —Elizabeth Barrett Browning

A Little Guide to Kindness

Kindness is helping out a stranger or traveller who needs assistance.

Kindness is extending the same courtesy to family, friends, and neighbors that is shown to others, instead of taking loved ones for granted.

Kindness is treating those in different or difficult circumstances with patience, respect, and understanding.

Kindness is offering comfort or cheer to someone who is lonely, ill, bereaved, or depressed—with a visit, a card, or a telephone call.

Kindness is making an extra effort to be patient and courteous in stressful situations—at work, in traffic, on the telephone.

Kindness is being friendly and always ready with a smile, a greeting, an introduction, or an acknowledgment.

Kindness is taking time to be positive—remembering to say "thank you" or giving someone praise, compliments, encouragement, and appreciation.

Kindness is being thoughtful—surprising someone with a token or expression of affection when it's not a special occasion—sending a card or flowers, giving a small gift, doing a little favor, preparing a special meal or treat.

Kindness is listening to someone's problems without passing judgment—giving someone "tea and sympathy" rather than unwanted advice or criticism.

Kindness is giving a caregiver a needed break—running an errand or taking a turn at a "relief" shift.

Kindness is showing consideration for others—holding a door, cleaning up for the next person, making sure that behavior is appropriate.

Kindness is treating the earth and everything living on it with care and consideration—being kind to animals and the environment.

Kindness is taking time to do something "extra" or "beyond" to help someone—forwarding mail, transferring a call, returning a lost object, volunteering to help.

Kindness is doing what isn't actually required, but what is truly needed.

—Jill Wolf